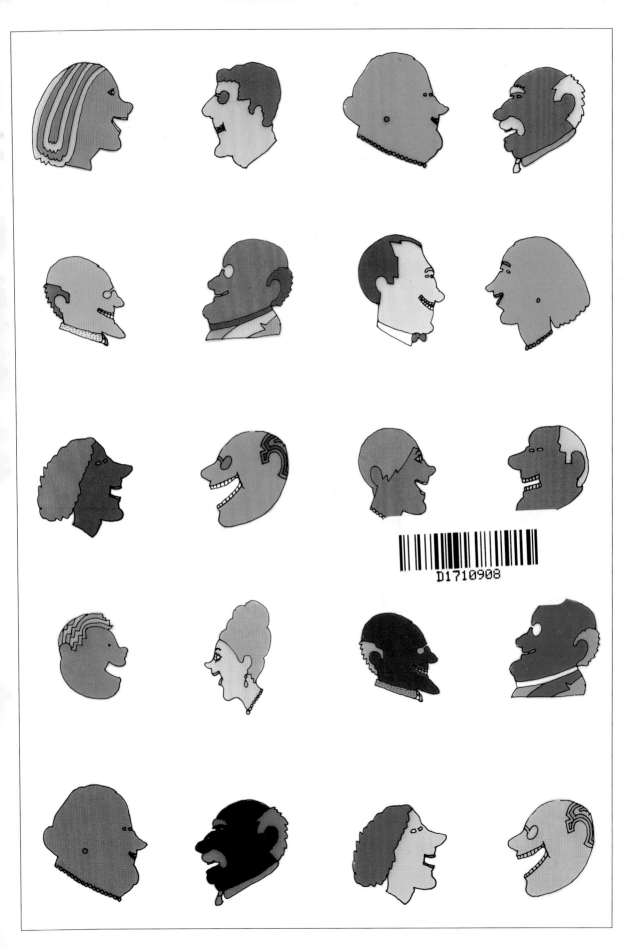

The Friendship Book

Charles Schulz

The Friendship Book

**A Festival of Fun, Beauty and Inspiration
For Every Kind of Friend**

Edited by Paul R. Wagner
Illustrated With a Colorful Collection
Of Photography, Stitchery, Graphic Poetry, Cartoon Strips
And Fine Art by a Variety of Artists

♛ Hallmark Crown Editions

The Friendship Book

Susan Tinker

You've Got a Friend

You just call out my name
And you know wherever I am
I'll come runnin' to see you again.
Winter, spring, summer or fall
All you have to do is call
And I'll be there. You've got a friend.

Carole King

What Is a Friend?

What is a Friend? I'll tell you.
It is a person with whom you dare to be yourself.
Your soul can go naked with him.
He seems to ask you to put on nothing,
   only to be what you really are.
When you are with him, you do not have to be on your guard.
You can say what you think, so long as it is genuinely you.
He understands those contradictions in
   your nature that cause others to misjudge you.
With him you breathe freely — you can allow
   your little vanities and envies and
        absurdities and in opening them up to him
   they are dissolved on the white ocean of his loyalty.
He understands. — You can weep with him,
   laugh with him, pray with him — through
   and underneath it all he sees, knows and loves you.
A Friend — I repeat — *is one with whom you dare to be yourself.*

Anonymous

Today
   I must breathe
      the words
         into my soul
LIVIN'
   is
      GIVIN'
and you
...you're a midwife of life

Joanne Ginsberg

Friendship

Oh, the comfort — the inexpressible comfort
  of feeling safe with a person.
Having neither to weigh thoughts,
Nor measure words — but pouring them
All right out — just as they are —
Chaff and grain together —
Certain that a faithful hand will
Take and sift them —
Keep what is worth keeping —
And with the breath of kindness
Blow the rest away.

Dinah Maria Mulock Craik

Arlene Noel

In Honor of Friendship

Two friends lived on adjoining lands — one alone, and the other with his wife and children. They harvested their grain, and one night the man without a family awoke and looked on his sheaves stacked beside him.

"How good God has been to me," he thought, "but my friend with his family needs more grain than I." So he carried some of his store to his friend's field.

And the other, surveying his own harvest, thought: "How much I have to enrich my life. How lonely my friend must be with so little of this world's joys."

So he arose and carried some of his grain and placed it on his friend's stack.

And in the morning when they went forth to glean again, each saw his heap of sheaves undiminished.

The exchange continued until one night in the moonlight the friends met, each with his arms filled on the way to the other's field. At the point where they met, the legend says, *a temple was built.*

Folk Tradition

from **The Star-Splitter**

If one by one we counted people out
For the least sin, it wouldn't take us long
To get so we had no one left to live with.
For to be social is to be forgiving.

Robert Frost

Seymour Chwast

The Abominable Snowman

I've never seen an abominable snowman,
I'm hoping not to see one,
I'm also hoping, if I do,
That it will be a wee one.

Ogden Nash

Friendship is related to love, and if love is the bread of life, friendship is in the same package. And friendship is a very good guide. In fact, it seems to me the world situation, as I write, is partially due to a lack of willingness to make friends, to care about other people, other lands. This characterizes the rulers of many countries. If the nations could work at making friends, there would be no threat of war, ever again.

I could not rewrite history, of course, but I could let friendship be a guidepost for my life.

Gladys Taber

To My Friend

I have never been rich before,
   But you have poured
Into my heart's high door
   A golden hoard.

My wealth is the vision shared,
   The sympathy,
The feast of the soul prepared
   By you for me.

Together we wander through
   The wooded ways.
Old beauties are green and new
   Seen through your gaze.

I look for no greater prize
   Than your soft voice.
The steadiness of your eyes
   Is my heart's choice.

I have never been rich before,
   But divine
Your steps on my sunlit floor
   And wealth is mine!

Anne Campbell

If I Had Known

If I had known what trouble you were bearing;
What griefs were in the silence of your face,
I would have been more gentle, and more caring,
And tried to give you gladness for a space.
I would have brought more warmth into the place,
    If I had known.

If I had known what thoughts despairing drew you;
(Why do we never try to understand?)
I would have lent a little friendship to you,
And slipped my hand within your hand,
And made your stay more pleasant in the land,
    If I had known.

Mary Carolyn Davies

FRIENDS ARE FOREVER GIVING

FRI ARE FOREVER GIVING LIFE
FRI ARE FOREVER GIVING LIFE
FRI ARE FOR GIV LIFE
FRI ARE FOREVER GIVING LIFE
FRI ARE FOREVER GIVING LIFE
FRI ARE FOR GIV LIFE
FRIENDS ARE FOR GIVING
FRIENDS ARE FOR GIVING IF

17

Paul R. Wagner and William M. Gilmore

Will You Be My Friend?

Will you be my friend?
There are so many reasons why you never should:
I'm sometimes sullen, often shy, acutely sensitive,
My fear erupts as anger, I find it hard to give,
I talk about myself when I'm afraid
And often spend a day without anything to say.
    But I will make you laugh
    And love you quite a bit
    And hold you when you're sad.
I cry a little almost every day
Because I'm more caring than the strangers ever know,
And, if at times, I show my tender side
(The soft and warmer part I hide)
    I wonder,
    Will you be my friend?
A friend
    Who far beyond the feebleness of any vow or tie
    Will touch the secret place where I am really I,
    To know the pain of lips that plead and eyes that weep,
    Who will not run away when you find me in the street
    Alone and lying mangled by my quota of defeats
    But will stop and stay — to tell me of another day
    When I was beautiful.

Will you be my friend?
There are so many reasons why you never should:
Often I'm too serious, seldom predictably the same,
Sometimes cold and distant, probably I'll always change.

I bluster and brag, seek attention like a child,
I brood and pout, my anger can be wild,
    But I will make you laugh
    And love you quite a bit
    And be near when you're afraid.
I shake a little almost every day
Because I'm more frightened than the strangers ever know
And if at times I show my trembling side
(The anxious, fearful part I hide)
    I wonder,
    Will you be my friend?
A friend
    Who, when I fear your closeness, feels me push away
    And stubbornly will stay to share what's left on such a day,
Who, when no one knows my name or calls me on the phone,
When there's no concern for me — what I have or haven't done —
And those I've helped and counted on have, oh so deftly, run,
Who, when there's nothing left but me, stripped
    of charm and subtlety,
Will nonetheless remain.

Will you be my friend?
    For no reason that I know
    Except I want you so.

James Kavanaugh

Tracy McVay

If You Want a Friend, Tame Me...

In Antoine de Saint-Exupéry's story
"THE LITTLE PRINCE," a small visitor from a distant planet
lands on the earth and travels in search of understanding.
This conversation between the little prince and a fox
he meets shows in a charming yet profound way how friends
are discovered — and what true friendship can mean.

"Good morning," said the fox.

"Good morning," the little prince responded politely.

"Who are you?" asked the little prince, and added, "You are very pretty to look at."

"I am a fox," the fox said.

"Come and play with me," proposed the little prince. "I am so unhappy."

"I cannot play with you," the fox said. "I am not tamed."

"Ah! Please excuse me," said the little prince.

But after some thought, he added:

"What does that mean — 'tame'?"

"It is an act too often neglected," said the fox. "It means to establish ties."

"'To establish ties'?"

"Just that," said the fox. "To me, you are still nothing more than a little boy who is just like a hundred thousand other little boys. And I have no need of you. And you, on your part, have no need of me. To you, I am nothing more than a fox like a hundred thousand other foxes. But if you tame me, then we shall need each other. To me, you will be unique in all the world. To you, I shall be unique in all the world....

"If you tame me, it will be as if the sun came to shine on my life. I shall know the sound of a step that will be different from all the others. Other steps send me hurrying back underneath the ground. Yours will call me, like music, out of my burrow. And then look: you see the grainfields down yonder? I do not eat bread. Wheat is of no use to me. The wheat fields have nothing to say to me. And that is sad. But you have hair that is the color of gold. Think how wonderful that will be when you have tamed me! The grain, which is also golden, will bring me back the thought of you. And I shall love to listen to the wind in the wheat...."

The fox gazed at the little prince, for a long time.

"Please — tame me!" he said.

"I want to, very much," the little prince replied. "But I have not much time. I have friends to discover, and a great many things to understand."

"One only understands the things that one tames," said the fox. "Men have no more time to understand anything. They buy things all ready made at the shops. But there is no shop anywhere where one can buy friendship, and so men have no friends any more. If you want a friend, tame me...."

Companion

Sometimes I feel a little like a god,
and other times, just
another man.
But never only what they think I am.
Again and again I labor
so long,
to make a companion
worthy of the greatest dream, the most
I've ever had.

If in my place he might speak,
answer only once,
I'd no longer worry
about the truth,
I'd settle for my companion.

Daniel Dahlquist

I Seem to Be/But Really I Am

My friends think I'm not equal
But I know I'm as good
My friends think that I'm not as smart as them
But I know I am.
Everybody thinks I hate cities
But I couldn't live on a farm
My parents think I hate my brother
But I couldn't do without him
Some think I can't run as fast or throw as far
But I know I can
Most people do not think I am an animal lover
But that is what has kept me up
My brother and sister don't think I will succeed
But I know I will.
Most people think if one of my friends is gone he's gone
But really my best friend saves me every time he talks.
Most people just think that I think the situation is bad
But I know it's horrible.
Many think I don't care
But really I want the world to be one family.

Jeff Morley

I wish

I wish I had a diamond
I wish I had a bike
I wish I had a cat
I wish I had a puppy
I wish I had a friend

Richard Ulloa
Student p. s. 61
new york city

All Losses Restored

When to the sessions of sweet silent thought
I summon up remembrance of things past,
I sigh the lack of many a thing I sought,
And with old woes new wail my dear time's waste:
Then can I drown an eye, unused to flow,
For precious friends hid in death's dateless night,
And weep afresh love's long since cancell'd woe,
And moan the expense of many a vanish'd sight:
Then can I grieve at grievances foregone,
And heavily from woe to woe tell o'er
The sad account of fore-bemoaned moan,
Which I new pay as if not paid before.
But if the while I think on thee, dear friend,
All losses are restored and sorrows end.

William Shakespeare

"He is my friend," I said —
"Be patient!" Overhead
  The skies were drear and dim;
  And lo! the thought of him
  Smiled on my heart — and then
  The sun shone out again!

James Whitcomb Riley

Ed Cooper

As I love Nature, as I love singing birds, and gleaming stubble, and flowing rivers, and morning and evening, and summer and winter, I love thee, my Friend.

Henry David Thoreau

Everything around us, a favorite chair, a book, a flower, is a patient companion who, unlike any other friend, faithfully waits for the time when we will need it.

Mary Dawson Hughes

To Look at Any Thing

To look at any thing,
If you would know that thing,
You must look at it long:
To look at this green and say
'I have seen spring in these
Woods,' will not do — you must
Be the thing you see:
You must be the dark snakes of
Stems and ferny plumes of leaves,
You must enter in
To the small silences between
The leaves,
You must take your time
And touch the very peace
They issue from.

John Moffitt

Steve Carter

from **The Diary of Anne Frank**

Saturday, 20 June, 1942

I haven't written for a few days, because I wanted first of all to think about my diary. It's an odd idea for someone like me to keep a diary; not only because I have never done so before, but because it seems to me that neither I — nor for that matter anyone else — will be interested in the unbosomings of a thirteen-year-old schoolgirl. Still, what does that matter? I want to write, but more than that, I want to bring out all kinds of things that lie buried deep in my heart.

There is a saying that "paper is more patient than man"; it came back to me on one of my slightly melancholy days, while I sat chin in hand, feeling too bored and limp even to make up my mind whether to go out or stay at home. Yes, there is no doubt that paper is patient and as I don't intend to show this cardboard-covered notebook, bearing the proud name of "diary," to anyone, unless I find a real friend, boy or girl, probably nobody cares. And now I come to the root of the matter, the reason for my starting a diary: it is that I have no such real friend.

Let me put it more clearly, since no one will believe that a girl of thirteen feels herself quite alone in the world, nor is it so. I have darling parents and a sister of sixteen. I know about thirty people whom one might call friends — I have strings of boy friends, anxious to catch a glimpse of me and who, failing that, peep at me through mirrors in class. I have relations, aunts and uncles, who are darlings too, a good home, no — I don't seem to lack anything. But it's the same with all my friends, just fun and joking, nothing more. I can never bring myself to talk of anything outside the common round. We don't seem to be able to get any closer, that is the root of the trouble. Perhaps I lack confidence, but anyway, there it is, a stubborn fact and I don't seem to be able to do anything about it.

Hence, this diary. In order to enhance in my mind's eye the picture of the friend for whom I have waited so long, I don't want to set down a series of bald facts in a diary like most people do, but I want this diary itself to be my friend, and I shall call my friend Kitty.

Anne Frank

from **I Have Found Such Joy**

I have found such joy in simple things;
A plain clean room, a nut-brown loaf of bread,
A cup of milk, a kettle as it sings,
The shelter of a roof above my head,
And in a leaf-laced square along a floor,
Where yellow sunlight glimmers through a door.

I have found such joy in things that fill
My quiet days: a curtain's blowing grace,
A potted plant upon my window sill,
A rose fresh-cut and placed within a vase,
A table cleared, a lamp beside a chair,
And books I long have loved beside me there.

Grace Noll Crowell

What sweetness is left in life, if you take away friendship? Robbing life of friendship is like robbing the world of the sun.

Cicero

Baking Soda

hooray for bakin' soda
ain't it neat
and cheers for
national bakin' soda week
for folks that's young
and folks that's old
bicarbonate of soda
will cure that cold
it cleans your teeth
and prevents the flu
and you can use it
in your car battery too
it puts out fires
of fat or grease
pass the bakin' soda
please
now
if your biscuits
cakes or pies
absolutely refuse
to rise
get the stuff
that's always slick
that bakin' soda
does the trick
and if you're feeling
far from placid
from an over excess
of stomach acid

just step right up and yell
don't stammer
get a big mess
of that arm and hammer
and if you cannot
clean your dentures
with any other
commercial ventures
from Portland Maine
to North Dakota
smart folks dunk
in bakin' soda
but beware your fun you botch
this ain't the kind
you mix with scotch

John Hartford

Donni Giambrone

Once, after puzzling long over the charm of Homer, I applied to a learned friend and said to him, "Can you tell me why Homer is so interesting?" "Well," said my friend, "Homer looked long at a thing. Do you know that if you should hold up your thumb and look at it long enough, you would find it immensely interesting?"

George Herbert Palmer

Ointment and perfume rejoice the heart: so doth the sweetness of a man's friend by hearty counsel.

Proverbs 27:9

Lighted Lamp

*Many of Vincent van Gogh's paintings
reflect his yearning for companionship.
The arrival of his friend, the painter
Paul Gauguin, brought hope of ending
Vincent's lonely days. But the strong
personalities of the two artists clashed
and Gauguin was forced to leave.
Vincent's painting* Gauguin's Chair
*recalls that famous visit and remains
as a symbol of van Gogh's need
and understanding of friendship.*

Love is something eternal — the aspect
may change, but not the essence. There
is the same difference in a person be-
fore and after he is in love as there is
in an unlighted lamp and one that is
burning. The lamp was there and it
was a good lamp, but now it is shedding
light, too, and that is its real function.

Vincent van Gogh

Such is friendship that through it we love places and seasons; for as bright bodies emit rays to a distance, and flowers drop their sweet leaves on the ground around them, so friends impart favor even to the places where they dwell. With friends even poverty is pleasant. Words cannot express the joy which a friend imparts; they only can know who have experienced that joy. A friend is dearer than the light of heaven, for it would be better for us that the sun were extinguished than that we should be without friends.

St. John Chrysostom

Winter Friendship

I get to know
trees
best in winter when
they stand out stark
against white snow.

In summer
it is as if we are
perhaps
at a gala affair —
joyfully aware of
each other's presence
without occasion for
deeper acquaintance.

But in winter
pinoak's pole-straight trunk
and wildly erratic branches
stand plainly revealed
like the supremely elegant
vase-shape of elm's
symmetric crown.
The garnet bark of the cherry
the ghostly gray dimensions
of great beeches
imprint themselves in my
awareness.

And the trees'
winter self-revelations
make me wonder
if you and I
stripped ourselves of the
dense minutiae of daily habit
might we not get to know
each other
    better?

Margaret Tsuda

Tom di Grazia

Delighted With Bluepink

Flowers! My friend, be delighted with what
you like; but with *something*.

Be delighted with something. Yesterday for
me it was watching sun on stones; wet stones.

I spent the morning lost in the wonder of
that. A delight of god's size.

The gods never saw anything more enchanting
than that. Gorgeous! the sun on wet stones.

But today what delights me is thinking of
bluepink flowers! Not that I've seen any...

Actually there isn't a flower of any kind
in the house — except in my head.

But, my friend, oh my friend! what wonderful
bluepink flowers! Delight in my bluepink flowers!

Kenneth Patchen

I Saw in Louisiana a Live-Oak Growing

I saw in Louisiana a live-oak growing,
All alone stood it and the moss hung down from the branches,
Without any companion it grew there uttering joyous leaves of dark green,
And its look, rude, unbending, lusty, made me think of myself,
But I wonder'd how it could utter joyous leaves
    standing alone there without its friend near, for I knew I could not,
And I broke off a twig with a certain number of leaves upon it,
    and twined around it a little moss,
And brought it away, and I have placed it in sight in my room,
It is not needed to remind me as of my own dear friends,
(For I believe lately I think of little else than of them,)
Yet it remains to me a curious token, it makes me think of manly love;
For all that, and though the live-oak glistens there in Louisiana
    solitary in a wide flat space,
Uttering joyous leaves all its life without a friend a lover near,
I know very well I could not.

Walt Whitman

Small Things

Blessed is the man who can enjoy the small things, the common beauties, the little day-by-day events; sunshine on the fields, birds on the bough, breakfast, dinner, supper, the daily paper on the porch, a friend passing by. So many people who go afield for enjoyment leave it behind them at home.

David Grayson

...damn everything that is grim, dull,
motionless, unrisking, inward turning,
damn everything that won't get into the
circle, that won't enjoy, that won't
throw its heart into the tension,
    surprise, fear and delight
    of the circus,
    the round world,
    the full existence...

S. Helen Kelley

Damn everything but the circus!

e. e. cummings

Norman LaLiberté

Dog and Man

Hours have passed. You have sat bent over your work. Following your searching, winging thoughts, your glance turns up and aside. There your eyes meet two other eyes, which, who shall say how long already or why, have been watching you from the depths of the chair in which your friend is curled up. No sound, no movement, nothing but two pair of eyes which in the buzzing silence of the room meet, and in that meeting become aware of unexpected happiness. He wags his tail, scarcely perceptibly, but immovably he keeps looking at you, with persistent gentleness, as if he feared that by and by immeasurable seas will separate him from you again.

But these wide seas. They separate you even now, gulfs of spiritual and bodily differences not to be bridged. You are indeed out of each other's reach and yet, at the same time, touchingly near. You ask for miracles; here is one of the miracles surrounding you which you so carelessly pass by. For is not this wonder greater than the meeting of two souls who can measure each other's virtues and needs in the depths of their own hearts?

This is the meeting of two souls flying to each other from two worlds which are irrevocably separated, different in kind, in aim, and destination. And yet, just as a power that moves the universe rushes through the infinite, incalculable distances, so a small spark of that same power can do away with all distances and separations between two beings and kindle the desire for warmth in their hearts.

Roland Holst

A Friend Indeed

...The cat is a philosophical, methodical, quiet animal, tenacious of his own habits, fond of order and cleanliness, and does not lightly confer his friendship. If you are worthy of his affection, a cat will be your friend but never your slave. He makes himself the companion of your hours of solitude, melancholy and toil. He will remain for whole evenings on your knee, uttering a contented purr, happy to be with you. Put him down and he will jump up again with a sort of cooing sound like a gentle reproach; and sometimes he will sit upon the carpet in front of you looking at you with eyes so melting, so caressing and so human, that they almost frighten you, for it is impossible to believe that a soul is not there.

Théophile Gautier

Chic Young

The only way to have a friend is to be one.

Ralph Waldo Emerson

To be a friend a man should start by being
a friend to himself.

Wilferd A. Peterson

Myself

I have to live with myself, and so
I want to be fit for myself to know.
I want to be able as days go by
Always to look myself in the eye.

I don't want to stand with the setting sun
And hate myself for the thing I've done.
I never can hide myself from me,
I see what others may never see.

I know what others may never know,
I never can fool myself, and so
Whatever happens I want to be
Self-respecting and conscience-free.

Edgar A. Guest

Very little is needed to make a happy life. It is all within yourself, in your way of thinking.

Marcus Aurelius

Be happy with what you have and are, be generous with both, and you won't have to hunt for happiness.

William E. Gladstone

You can within yourself find a mighty, unexplored kingdom in which you can dwell in peace if you will.

Russell H. Conwell

STEINBERG

If there's a stranger in your neighbor-
hood today, better check up on him;
he may need a friend. If he's still a
stranger tomorrow, better check up on
your neighborhood.

Burton Hillis

If it is a virtue to love my neighbor as a human being, it must be a virtue — and not a vice — to love myself, since I am a human being too.

Erich Fromm

Where Are You?

O, your warmest friend,
    little fish,
was right there in
    your heart
and you didn't even
    know it —
What did you do
    to him?
he won't come out now
and I don't know where
    he is —
BUT,
if you find him,
tell him about us
'cause he's the one we'd
REALLY LIKE TO MEET.

Paul R. Wagner

To give life a meaning one must have
a purpose larger than one's self.

Will Durant

Fred Klemushin

This above all: to thine own self be true,
And it must follow, as the night the day,
Thou canst not then be false to any man.

William Shakespeare

Love Thy Neighbour as Thyself.

Leviticus 19:18

If you love yourself, you love everybody else as you do yourself. As long as you love another person less than you love yourself, you will not really succeed in loving yourself, but if you love all alike, including yourself, you will love them as one person and that person is both God and man. Thus he is a great and righteous person who, loving himself, loves all others equally.

Meister Eckhart

Fernando Casini

Whoever Finds This - I Love You

On a quiet street in the city, a little old man walked along.
Shufflin' thru the autumn afternoon.
And the autumn leaves reminded him
Another summer's come and gone.
He had a lonely night ahead waitin' for June.
Then among the leaves near the orphan's home,
A piece of paper caught his eye.
And he stooped to pick it up with trembling hands.
As he read the childish writing the old man began to cry.
'Cause the words burned inside him like a brand.
Whoever finds this, I love you.
Whoever finds this, I need you.
I ain't got no one to talk to
So whoever finds this I love you.

The old man's eyes searched the orphan's home
And came to rest upon a child
With her nose pressed up against the windowpane.
And the old man knew he'd found a friend at last.
So he waved at her and smiled.
And they both knew they'd spend the winter
Laughin' at the rain.
And they did spend the winter laughing at the rain.
Talkin' thru the trees and exchanging little gifts
They'd made for each other.
The old man would carve toys for the little girl,
And she would draw pictures for him of beautiful ladies
Surrounded by green trees and sunshine,
And they laughed a lot.
But then on the first day of June,
The little girl ran to the fence to show the old man
A picture she'd drawn, but he wasn't there.

And somehow, the little girl knew he wasn't coming back.
So she went back to her room, took a crayon,
Piece of paper, and wrote:
Whoever finds this, I love you.
Whoever finds this, I need you.
I ain't even got no one to talk to
So whoever finds this I love you.

Mac Davis

The Mirror of Friendship

Friendship brings out the best in people, even rising above language barriers, as related in this personal experience by Elizabeth Mauske.

On her frequent trips on foot to Temuco, an old Araucanian Indian woman used always to bring my mother a few partridge eggs or a handful of berries. My mother spoke no Araucanian beyond the greeting *"Mai-mai,"* and the old woman knew no Spanish, but she drank tea and ate cake with many an appreciative giggle. We girls stared fascinated at her layers of colorful hand-woven clothing, her copper bracelets and coin necklaces, and we vied with each other in trying to memorize the singsong phrase she always spoke on rising to leave.

At last we learned the words by heart and repeated them to the missionary, who translated them for us. They have stayed in my mind as the nicest compliment ever uttered:

"I shall come again, for I like myself when I'm near you."

David Hamilton

When we start at the center of ourselves, we discover something worthwhile extending toward the periphery of the circle. We find again some of the joy in the now, some of the peace in the here, some of the love in me and thee which go to make up the kingdom of heaven on earth.

Anne Morrow Lindbergh

Set in Goudy Old Style with display type
in Goudy Old Style Bold, a delicately styled
original alphabet drawn by the American designer
Frederic W. Goudy for the Monotype in 1905.
Printed on Hallmark Crown Royale Book paper.
Designed by William M. Gilmore.